THE CIVIL WAR

THE NASHVILLE SESSIONS

Lyrics by JACK MURPHY   Music by FRANK WILDHORN

By FRANK WILDHORN, GREGORY BOYD and JACK MURPHY

WARNER BROS. PUBLICATIONS - THE GLOBAL LEADER IN PRINT
USA: 15800 NW 48th Avenue, Miami, FL 33014

WARNER/CHAPPELL MUSIC
CANADA: 40 SHEPPARD AVE. WEST, SUITE 800
TORONTO, ONTARIO, M2N 6K9
SCANDINAVIA: P.O. BOX 533, VENDEVAGEN 85 B
S-182 15, DANDERYD, SWEDEN
AUSTRALIA: P.O. BOX 353
3 TALAVERA ROAD, NORTH RYDE N.S.W. 2113

NUOVA CARISCH
ITALY: VIA CAMPANIA, 12
20098 S. GIULIANO MILANESE (MI)
ZONA INDUSTRIALE SESTO ULTERIANO
SPAIN: MAGALLANES, 25
28015 MADRID
FRANCE: 25 RUE DE HAUTEVILLE, 75010 PARIS

INTERNATIONAL MUSIC PUBLICATIONS LIMITED
ENGLAND: SOUTHEND ROAD,
WOODFORD GREEN, ESSEX IG8 8HN
GERMANY: MARSTALLSTR. 8, D-80539 MUNCHEN
DENMARK: DANMUSIK, VOGNMAGERGADE 7
DK 1120 KOBENHAVNK

Project Manager: Sy Feldman
Art Layout: Lisa Greene Mane

A Note from the Composer:

For the last two years, over 200 musicians, singers, actors, engineers and producers, coming from the worlds of theatre, opera, country, gospel, rock and R&B, have taken an idea to create a musical tapestry of our country's Civil War and turned it into the most incredible musical journey I've ever had the privilege of being a part of. The live, theatrical, musical experience that is THE CIVIL WAR begins its life at Houston's Alley Theatre (birthplace of JEKYLL & HYDE) this September, moves on to the famed Shubert Theatre in New Haven and opens on Broadway in the spring of '99. Like JEKYLL & HYDE and THE SCARLET PIMPERNEL before it, THE CIVIL WAR begins its life with these recordings.

As Greg, Jack and I began work on this piece, it became clear to us that its "musical vocabulary" could create a unique opportunity, one that would allow us to bring artists from so many musical styles together, bridging the worlds of theatre and popular music. The challenge was to make the music "real," not some "Broadway" version of the style but songs that these contemporary, popular artists would feel they could bring their own artistry to and yet retain the essence of the piece itself. Beyond my wildest dreams (and mine are pretty big!), some of my favorite artists came aboard and an amazing crew was assembled for the journey.

On this, "THE CIVIL WAR - THE NASHVILLE SESSIONS," Trace Adkins, John Berry, Deana Carter, Charlie Daniels, Linda Eder, Michael English, Amy Grant, Tracy Lawrence, Gene Miller, Kevin Sharp, Shiloh, Travis Tritt, Bryan White, BeBe Winans and Trisha Yearwood make these songs come alive with honesty, power, beauty and grace and make the characters they are portraying "live" within this vital story.

And so to all the artists, their representatives and record companies, and especially to mine here at Atlantic that I've had the pleasure of sharing this journey with, my gratitude beyond words. And to the listner, as always ...Enjoy!

All best,

Frank Wildhorn

1 PROLOGUE

CHARLIE DANIELS

On the twelfth of April, 1861, Confederate guns opened fire on Fort Sumter in Charleston Harbor, thus beginning the bloodiest conflict in American History -- 620,000 dead -- more than all other American wars combined. The Civil War remains this nation's single most defining experience, ultimately giving new meaning to the word Freedom. Walt Whitman, a young newspaperman destined to become America's greatest poet wrote: "Future years will never know the seething hell and the black infernal background of this war -- and it is best they should not -- the real war will never get in the books."

2 THE DAY THE SUN STOOD STILL

TRAVIS TRITT

This song is based on the writings of a Southern officer named Henry Kyd Douglas, an aide to General Stonewall Jackson. He was in a ferocious battle where it seemed to him that the day lasted forever (as if "the sun would never go down" to bring an end to the fighting).

WE WERE YOUNG AND BOUND FOR GLORY
ITCHIN' FOR A FIGHT LIKE YOU
BRINGIN' HELL AND PURGATORY
TO THE BOYS WHO WORE THE BLUE
AND I THOUGHT I'D SEEN IT ALL
TILL THE DAY NIGHT WOULDN'T FALL
OH HOW THE SUN DID BLAZE
WOULDN'T GO DOWN FOR DAYS
I GOT SHOT AND LOST MY RIFLE
WHEN THE FIRST WAVE HIT THE RISE
AND THE GUNS ROLLED OUT LIKE THUNDER
AND THE BLACK SMOKE BURNED MY EYES
AND I WATCHED IT ALL UNFOLD
JUST THE WAY THE BIBLE TOLD
JOSHUA'S ENDLESS DAY
KEEPIN' THE NIGHT AT BAY
AND THE SOLDIERS KEPT A' COMIN'
TILL THE GROUND LOOKED LIKE A SEA
OF BLUE AND GRAY
AND I WATCHED THEM FROM A DISTANCE
WONDRIN' IF I WOULD'VE FOUGHT OR RUN AWAY
THE DAY THE SUN STOOD STILL
HOW THEY BEAT THE BLOODY DRUMS
AND THE SECONDS MOVED LIKE HOURS
BUT THE SUNSET NEVER COMES
AND THE CANNONS SHAKE THE GROUND
AND THE BULLETS TEST YOUR WILL
EVEN SHADOWS FOUND NO COVER
ON THAT GODFORSAKEN HILL
THE DAY THE SUN STOOD STILL
AND I WATCHED THEM LEAN THEIR SHOULDERS
TO THE FEARFUL HAIL OF LEAD
AND I PRAYED FOR NIGHT TO SAVE US
AND I CRIED AND BOWED MY HEAD
BUT THE SUN JUST KEPT A' CREEPIN'
'CROSS A COLD INDIFFERENT SKY
CASTIN' A DEADLY GLOW
ON ALL THE MEN BELOW
ALL THE HOURS IN A LIFETIME
DON'T ADD UP TO ONE WHOLE MINUTE
IN THAT SUN
AND THE HEROES AND THE COWARDS
LOOK THE SAME WHEN THEY HAVE FALLEN
BY THE GUN
THE DAY THE SUN STOOD STILL
AND THE NORTH AND SOUTH LOOKED WEST
BUT THE EVENING STAR WAS SLEEPING
AND THE DAYLIGHT WOULDN'T REST
OUT ON THE KILLING FLOOR
THE RED SUN ON THE HILL
SHININ' DOWN ON ALL THE DEAD MEN
WITH A STRANGE AND EERIE CHILL
THE DAY THE SUN STOOD STILL
DO NOT JUDGE WHAT YOUR BROTHER DOES
TILL YOU'VE WALKED A MILE
RANK BY BLOODY FILE
WHO'S TO SAY IF YOU'LL RUN OR STAY
AND FIGHT?
THE DAY THE SUN STOOD STILL
IS JUST BENEATH THE SKIN
IN THE SOUL OF EVERY SOLDIER
EVERY BATTLE THAT HE'S IN
THE DAY THE SUN STOOD STILL
WILL HAUNT YOUR DREAMS AT NIGHT
AND STALK YOUR EVERY SUNRISE
THOUGH YOU WILL NOT KNOW IT TILL
THE DAY THE SUN STANDS STILL
HOW THEY'LL BEAT THE BLOODY DRUMS
AND THE SECONDS MOVE LIKE HOURS
BUT THE SUNSET NEVER COMES
AND THE CANNONS SHAKE THE GROUND
AND THE BULLETS TEST YOUR WILL
EVEN SHADOWS FIND NO COVER
ON SOME GODFORSAKEN HILL ON
THE DAY THE SUN STOOD STILL

3 MISSING YOU (MY BILL)

DEANA CARTER

The young wife of an absent Union officer writes to her husband of her daily, lonely struggle to hold their family together.

I LEARNED TO CHOP A TREE TODAY
I LAUGHED SO HARD I CRIED
AND BILLY HELPED AND SCRAPED HIS KNEE
BUT HE TOOK IT ALL IN STRIDE
DAY BY DAY I GET BY
MAKIN' DO THE BEST I CAN
WHEN THE SUN SLOWLY SETS
JUST BEHIND OUR HILL
THEN THE MEMORIES COME
IN THE EVENING CHILL
HOW I LONG FOR YOUR TOUCH
LIKE A LOVER WILL
OH, I'M MISSIN' YOU
GOD, I'M MISSIN' YOU ...
MY BILL
THE PARLOR ROOF STILL LEAKS A BIT
WHERE THE GABLE MEETS THE EVE
YOU ALWAYS MEANT TO GET TO IT
BUT I KNOW YOU HAD TO LEAVE
THANK GOD THERE'S SO MUCH TO DO
IT'S THE WORK THAT GETS ME THROUGH
WHEN THE SUN SLOWLY SETS
JUST BEHIND OUR HILL
THEN THE MEMORIES COME
IN THE EVENING CHILL
HOW I LONG FOR YOUR TOUCH
LIKE A LOVER WILL
OH, I'M MISSIN' YOU
GOD, I'M MISSIN' YOU ...
MY BILL
SO I COUNT THE DAYS
AND I THINK UP WAYS
TO SPEED THEM BY
BUT WHEN THE DAY IS THROUGH
I REMEMBER YOU AND CRY
WHEN THE SUN SLOWLY SETS
JUST BEHIND OUR HILL
THEN THE MEMORIES COME
IN THE EVENING CHILL
HOW I LONG FOR YOUR TOUCH
LIKE A LOVER WILL
OH, I'M MISSIN' YOU
GOD, I'M MISSIN' YOU ...
MY BILL

4 VIRGINIA

GENE MILLER

A Captain in General Lee's fabled Army of Northern Virginia, wistfully remembering a time gone by, sings an anthem of patriotism for the "country" he loves.

THERE WAS A TIME ...
A TIME OF SPLENDOR AND GRACE
WHEN THE WORLD MOVED BY
AT A KINDER PACE
THERE WAS A LAND ...
A LAND TO PLEASURE THE EYES
WHERE THE OLD WAS NEW
AND THE FOOLISH WISE
I CAN HEAR VIRGINIA
WHEN THE SOUTH WIND SINGS
AND I SEE HER SHINING
ON A BLACKBIRD'S SILVER WINGS
AND I CAN FEEL VIRGINIA
RUNNIN' THROUGH MY SOUL
WHEN THE FLAG UNFURLS
AND THE DRUMMERS START THEIR LONG, LONG ROLL
OH, SACRED GROUND
FOR WHICH SO MANY HAVE DIED
LET US TAKE OUR TURN
FOR OUR COUNTRY'S PRIDE
OH, BLESSED PLACE
REMEMBER ALL OF YOUR SONS
WHO WILL STAND AND FALL
'NEATH THE CEASELESS GUNS
I CAN HEAR VIRGINIA
WHEN THE SOUTH WIND SINGSAND I SEE HER SHINING
ON A BLACKBIRD'S SILVER WINGS
AND I CAN FEEL VIRGINIA
RUNNIN' THROUGH MY SOUL
WHEN THE FLAG UNFURLS
AND THE DRUMMERS START THEIR LONG, LONG ROLL
WILL I EVER SEE HER RISE AGAIN?
OR ARE THE OLD DAYS GONE,
HAS THE WORLD MOVED ON?
WILL SHE EVER GRACE OUR EYES AGAIN?
TELL ME WHEN?
I CAN HEAR VIRGINIA
WHEN THE SOUTH WIND SINGS
AND I SEE HER SHINING
ON A BLACKBIRD'S SILVER WINGS
AND I CAN FEEL VIRGINIA
RUNNIN' THROUGH MY SOUL
WHEN THE FLAG UNFURLS
AND THE DRUMMERS START THEIR LONG, LONG ROLL

5 OLD GRAY COAT

TRACE ADKINS

A grizzled Southern veteran sings the praises of his "old gray coat," a metaphor for his unswerving loyalty to the Confederacy.

WELL, THEY GAVE ME THIS OLD COAT
SAID "IT'LL KEEP YOU MIGHTY WARM
IT'LL SEE YOU THROUGH THE WINTER
IT'S YOUR 'BY GOD' UNIFORM!"
SO I WEAR IT EVERYDAY
AND I SLEEP IN IT AT NIGHT
NOW IT'S TWENTY SHADES OF GRAY
AND THE WAIST IS SHRUNK TOO TIGHT
AND THE BOTTOM'S CAKED AND MUDDY
AND THE BUTTONS ARE HALF GONE
BUT JUST LIKE YOU AND ME
THIS OLD GRAY COAT WEARS ON
AND WHEN I DIE IN THIS GRAY COAT
I'M GONNA' MARCH THROUGH HEAVEN'S DOOR
I'M GONNA' WALK UP TO ST. PETER
AND TELL HIM "SEND ME BACK FOR MORE"
CAUSE I'LL BE DAMNED IF I'LL JUST SIT AROUND
WHILE YOU BOYS WIN THE WAR
CAUSE EVEN WHEN I'M DEAD
SHOT FULL OF YANKEE LEAD
THERE'LL BE PART OF ME KEEPS
HANGIN' BY A THREAD ...
OF THIS OLD GRAY COAT
WHEN I THINK OF ALL THE PLACES
THIS OLD COAT AND ME HAVE BEEN
THROUGH THE FAT AND LEAN AND INBETWEEN
DOUBLE QUICK THROUGH THICK AND THIN
FROM THE BALLROOMS DOWN IN RICHMOND
TO THE TOP OF MARYE'S HEIGHTS
FROM MANASSAS TO THE WILDERNESS
AND A HUNDRED OTHER FIGHTS
NOW THE COLLAR'S TORN AND TATTERED
AND THE ELBOW'S WORN CLEAN THROUGH
BUT, BUDDY, IN A PINCH
THIS OLD GRAY COAT WILL DO
AND WHEN I DIE IN THIS GRAY COAT
AND WHEN THEY COME TO BURY ME
IF THEY COMMENCE TO SPEECHAFYIN'
AND SINGIN' "NEARER, LORD, TO THEE"
WELL, BE DAMN SURE I AIN'T JUST SLEEPIN'
CAUSE I FLAT OUT GUARANTEE
THAT EVEN WHEN I'M DEAD
SHOT FULL OF YANKEE LEAD
THAT THE TOUGHEST PART LIVES
ON IN EVERY SHRED ...
OF THIS OLD GRAY COAT
YOU CAN CUT MY THROAT
YOU CAN SINK MY BOAT
BUT YOU CAN NEVER STOP THIS OLD GRAY COAT
WHEN MY BONES YOU TOTE
WHEN THAT'S ALL SHE WROTE

I'LL FIGHT ON INSIDE THIS OLD GRAY COAT
CAUSE WHEN I DIE IN THIS GRAY COAT
I'M GONNA' MARCH THROUGH HEAVEN'S DOOR
I'M GONNA' WALK UP TO ST. PETER
AND TELL HIM "SEND ME BACK FOR MORE"
CAUSE I'LL BE DAMNED IF I'LL JUST SIT AROUND
WHILE YOU BOYS WIN THE WAR
CAUSE EVEN WHEN I'M DEAD
SHOT FULL OF YANKEE LEAD
THERE AIN'T NOTHIN' THAT
I'D RATHER WEAR INSTEAD ...
OF THIS OLD GRAY COAT
THIS OLD GRAY COAT
I'LL GO DOWN IN THIS OLD GRAY COAT
THIS OLD GRAY COAT.

6 I'LL NEVER PASS THIS WAY AGAIN

TRACY LAWRENCE

Everyman's lament at not having noticed the "ordinary days" until it's too late.

I WAS BORN BESIDE THIS RIVER
'BOUT A HALF A MILE FROM HERE
BUT I NEVER SEEMED TO NOTICE
THAT THE WATER RAN THIS CLEAR
AND I'VE NEVER SEEN THAT COLOR GREEN
SPARKLE DOWN THE GLEN
NOW I'LL NEVER PASS THIS WAY AGAIN
I HAVE WANDERED THROUGH THAT ORCHARD
AND PLAYED AMONG HER TREES
BUT I NEVER HEARD THE SECRETS
THAT SHE WHISPERS ON THE BREEZE
FOR THE ONLY SOUND ON HALLOWED GROUND
IS THE SILENCE OF THE MEN
WHO WILL NEVER PASS THIS WAY AGAIN
IT NEVER SHONE AS BEAUTIFUL
AS HOW IT LOOKS TODAY
WE NEVER MISS THE THINGS WE LOVE
'TIL THEY GO AWAY
BUT I HAVE HEARD THE BUGLER'S CALL
AND IT'S TIME FOR ME TO LEAVE
CAUSE THERE COMES A DAY WHEN A MAN MUST SAY
I WILL DIE FOR WHAT I BELIEVE
I HAVE OFTEN THROWN MY PENNIES
IN THAT OLD WISHING WELL
AND IF I HAD A PENNY
I WOULD WISH ME A SPELL
I WOULD KNEEL AND PRAY THAT HERE I'D STAY
FOREVER AMEN
BUT I'LL NEVER PASS THIS WAY
NO I'LL NEVER PASS THIS WAY
NO I'LL NEVER PASS THIS WAY AGAIN

7 RIVER JORDAN

BEBE WINANS

A group of slaves, in the privacy of the "quarters," sing hopefully of their deliverance.

WE BREAK OUR BACKS FOR THE MASTER'S PLEASURE
JUST WAITIN' FOR THE SWEET OLD BY AND BY
SINGIN' "GO DOWN MOSES" AT THE LEVEE
TILL WE LAY OUR BURDEN DOWN AND DIE
BUT THEY SAY THERE'S A NEW WIND BLOWIN'
DOWN BY THE MIGHTY MISSISSIPPI DRESSED IN BLUE
SHAKIN' LOOSE THESE CHAINS THAT BIND ME
TILL THIS ENDLESS NIGHT IS FINALLY THROUGH ... SO NOW
MEET ME BY THE RIVER JORDAN
KNEE-DEEP IN A RISIN' TIDE
WE WILL CLIMB ABOARD THAT BOAT CALLED FREEDOM
AND WE'LL ALL SAIL OVER TO THE OTHER SIDE
SAIL ON
JUST SAIL, SAIL ON
SAIL ON OVER TO THE OTHER SIDE
SAIL, SAIL ON
JUST SAIL ON
JUST SAIL ON OVER TO THE OTHER SIDE
MEET ME BY THE RIVER JORDAN
KNEE-DEEP IN A RISIN' TIDE
WE'LL CLIMB ABOARD THAT BOAT CALLED FREEDOM
AND WE'LL ALL SAIL ON OVER TO THE OTHER SIDE
WE'LL BE SINGIN' HALLELUJA
WHEN THIS MIS'RY SURE 'NOUGH BE PASSED
WE'LL BE SINGIN' HALLELUJAH
HALLELUJAH, WE ARE NOW FREE AT LAST
HOLD ON ... HOLD ON
WHEN YOU LIVE IN THE EAST OF EDEN
YOU'VE GOT TO PRAY
THAT YOU'LL FIND YOURSELF IN PARADISE ONE DAY
MEET ME BY THE RIVER JORDAN
KNEE-DEEP IN A RISIN' TIDE
WE'LL CLIMB ABOARD THAT BOAT CALLED FREEDOM
AND WE'LL ALL SAIL ON OVER TO THE OTHER SIDE
MEET ME BY THE RIVER JORDAN
KNEE-DEEP IN A RISIN' TIDE
WE'LL CLIMB ABOARD THAT BOAT CALLED FREEDOM
AND WE'LL SAIL RIGHT ON OVER TO THE OTHER SIDE
WE'LL BE SINGIN' HALLELUJAH
WHEN THIS MIS'RY SURE 'NOUGH BE PASSED
WE'LL BE SINGIN' HALLELUJAH
HALLELUJAH, WE ARE NOW FREE AT LAST
MEET ME BY THE RIVER JORDAN
KNEE-DEEP IN A RISIN' TIDE
WE'LL CLIMB ABOARD THAT BOAT CALLED FREEDOM
AND WE'LL ALL SAIL ON OVER TO THE OTHER SIDE
MEET ME BY THE RIVER JORDAN
KNEE-DEEP IN A RISIN' TIDE
WE'LL CLIMB ABOARD THAT BOAT CALLED FREEDOM
AND WE'LL SAIL RIGHT ON OVER TO THE OTHER SIDE
WE'LL BE SINGIN' HALLELUJAH
WHEN THIS MIS'RY SURE 'NOUGH BE PASSED
WE'LL BE SINGIN' HALLELUJAH
HALLELUJAH, WE ARE NOW FREE AT LAST
HOLD ON ... HOLD ON
WHEN YOU LIVE IN THE EAST OF EDEN
YOU'VE GOT TO PRAY
THAT YOU'LL FIND YOURSELF
IN PARADISE ONE DAY
MEET ME BY THE RIVER JORDAN
KNEE-DEEP IN A RISIN' TIDE
WE'LL CLIMB ABOARD
THAT BOAT CALLED FREEDOM
AND WE'LL ALL SAIL RIGHT ON OVER
TO THE OTHER SIDE.

8 WITH THESE HANDS

BRYAN WHITE AND AMY GRANT

A Confederate officer and his wife savor the precious moments of what both realize could be his final leave, their eternal love fired by the passion they both feel for each other.

LOOK AT THESE HANDS
THEY ARE BATTLE SCARRED AND WEARY
AND THEY'RE ACHIN' FOR THE ONE THING
THAT CAN HEAL THE PAIN
FOR THE FEEL OF YOU AT SUNDOWN
RUNNIN' FIRE THROUGH MY VEINS
LOOK AT THESE HANDS
THEY'VE BEEN HOLDIN' ON AND PRAYIN'
AND THEY'RE TREMBLING FOR YOUR QUIET,
EASY TOUCH
LOOK AT THESE HANDS REACHING OUT FOR THE MAN
I LOVE TOO MUCH
COME TO ME NOW
WHISPER SECRETS SOFT AND LOW
LAY HERE BESIDE ME
DARLIN' DON'T LET ME GO
WITH THESE HANDS I COULD HOLD YOU FOREVER
WITH THIS HEART I WILL ALWAYS BE TRUE
JUST LIKE GOD IN HIS HEAVEN
MAY YOU ALWAYS BE THERE
EVERY TIME THAT THESE HANDS REACH FOR YOU
LOOK AT THESE EYES
THEY HAVE SEEN SO MANY DEVILS
THEY CAN HARDLY RECOGNIZE THE ANGEL HERE
I ONLY KNOW WHEN I LOOK IN YOUR EYES
YOU CALM ALL MY FEARS
WE'VE GOT TONIGHT
DARLIN', WE CAN'T ASK FOR MORE
JUST HOLD ME TIGHT
LEAVE THE WORLD OUTSIDE THE DOOR
WITH THESE EYES I COULD SEE YOU FOREVER
WITH THIS HEART I WILL ALWAYS BE TRUE
LIKE THE STARS IN THE HEAVENS
MY LOVE WILL BE THERE
EVERY TIME THAT THESE EYES LOOK AT YOU
WITH THESE HANDS
WITH THESE EYES
WITH THIS HEART
I'LL BE THERE...
I'LL BE THERE...
WITH THESE HANDS I COULD HOLD YOU FOREVER
WITH THIS HEART I WILL ALWAYS BE TRUE
JUST LIKE GOD IN HIS HEAVEN
MAY YOU ALWAYS BE THERE
EVERY TIME THAT THESE HANDS REACH FOR YOU
JUST LIKE GOD IN HIS HEAVEN
MY LOVE WILL BE THERE
EVERY TIME THAT THESE HANDS REACH FOR YOU
EVERY TIME THAT THESE HANDS REACH FOR YOU

9 JUDGMENT DAY

SHILOH

(Gene Miller, John Porter McMeans and Denny Henson) A battle weary Confederate Captain faces the consequences of the field decisions he makes, on both the lives of his men, and the condition of his conscience.

... AND SOMETIMES IT'S TOO MUCH TO BEAR
THE DEAD AND DYING EVERYWHERE
AND EVERY DAY, FOR ME, IS JUDGMENT DAY
EVERY DAY, FOR ME, IS JUDGMENT DAY ...
I SIT AMONG MY CHARTS AND MAPS
AND HEAR THE LONELY CALL OF TAPS
LIKE THE WIND ACROSS THE MOON
I PRAY TO GOD THAT I AM RIGHT
AND THEN I SEND BOYS OFF TO FIGHT
AND TRAVEL HOME IN BOXES FAR TOO SOON
MAY GOD HAVE MERCY ON MY SOUL
FOR ALL THE YEARS THAT I HAVE STOLEN
FROM THE MEN WHO FOLLOW WHAT I SAY
AND MAY THEIR FAMILIES ALL FORGIVE
THE ORDERS I SO CALMLY GIVE THEM
AS I MARCH THEIR SONS INTO HARM'S WAY
AND OUT THERE ON THE KILLING FLOOR
I HEAR THE BLOODY SOUNDS OF WAR
AND WATCH A THOUSAND MORE SOULS SLIP AWAY
AND SOMETIMES IT'S TOO MUCH TO BEAR
THE DEAD AND DYING EVERYWHERE
AND EVERY DAY, FOR ME, IS JUDGMENT DAY
EVERY DAY, FOR ME, IS JUDGMENT DAY
I WRITE TO MOTHERS OF THEIR SONS
AND SAY "THEY WERE THE BRAVEST ONES"
AND THEN I POUR A DRINK AND SLEEP
BUT SLEEP IS ONLY FILLED WITH DRUMS
A SLICE OF DEATH TILL MORNING COMES
THE HEART OF DARKNESS
WHERE MY SOUL CAN WEEP
COME WALK A MILE IN BLOODY SHOES
AND LOSE THE MEN THAT I AM LOSING
WATCH THEM PAY THE PIPER FOR MY TUNE
COME WALK AMONG THEIR GHOSTS WITH ME
AND LOOK THROUGH EYES TOO USED TO SEEING
FACES WHO HAVE JOINED THE LOST PLATOON
COME JUDGMENT DAY GOD ONLY KNOWS
IF MAN WILL REAP THE PAIN HE SOWS
AND WHAT WILL BE THE PRICE HE HAS TO PAY
BUT DOWN HERE ON THE KILLING FLOOR
AMONG THE CRIMSON RAGS OF WAR
FOR ME, EACH DAY I LIVE IS JUDGMENT DAY
EVERY DAY, FOR ME, IS JUDGMENT DAY
MAY GOD HAVE MERCY ON MY SOUL
FOR ALL THE YEARS THAT I HAVE STOLEN
FROM THE MEN WHO FOLLOW WHAT I SAY
AND MAY THEIR FAMILIES ALL FORGIVE
THE ORDERS I SO CALMLY GIVE THEM
AS I MARCH THEIR SONS INTO HARM'S WAY
AND OUT THERE ON THE KILLING FLOOR
I HEAR THE BLOODY SOUNDS OF WAR
AND WATCH A THOUSAND MORE SOULS SLIP AWAY
AND SOMETIMES IT'S TOO MUCH TO BEAR
THE DEAD AND DYING EVERYWHERE
AND EVERY DAY, FOR ME, IS JUDGMENT DAY
EVERY DAY, FOR ME, IS JUDGMENT DAY
EVERY DAY, FOR ME, IS JUDGMENT DAY

10 TELL MY FATHER

KEVIN SHARP

A young Northern infantryman, mortally wounded in the war's first major encounter, begs his best friend to assure the dying boy's father that he acquitted himself with honor and upheld the family name. He lived as a boy and died as a man.

TELL MY FATHER THAT HIS SON
DIDN'T RUN, OR SURRENDER
THAT I BORE HIS NAME WITH PRIDE
AS I TRIED TO REMEMBER
YOU ARE JUDGED BY WHAT YOU DO
WHILE PASSING THROUGH
AS I REST 'NEATH FIELDS OF GREEN
LET HIM LEAN ON YOUR SHOULDER
TELL HIM HOW I SPENT MY YOUTH
SO THE TRUTH COULD GROW OLDER
TELL MY FATHER WHEN YOU CAN
I WAS A MAN
TELL HIM WE WILL MEET AGAIN
WHERE THE ANGELS LEARN TO FLY
TELL HIM WE WILL MEET AS MEN
FOR WITH HONOR DID I DIE
TELL HIM HOW I WORE THE BLUE
PROUD AND TRUE THROUGH THE FIRE
TELL MY FATHER SO HE'LL KNOW
I LOVE HIM SO
TELL HIM HOW I WORE THE BLUE
PROUD AND TRUE LIKE HE TAUGHT ME
TELL MY FATHER NOT TO CRY
THEN SAY GOOD-BYE

11 I NEVER KNEW HIS NAME

LINDA EDER

A nurse weeps under the weight of the nameless hundreds of young men she has seen cut down in the first bloom of life.

I NEVER KNEW HIS NAME
AS HE CALLED TO ME
PLEADING WITH HIS EYES
SUDDENLY SO WISE
TRYING NOT TO CRY
NOW HE'S GONE AND I
NEVER KNEW HIS NAME
I'VE SEEN HIS KIND BEFORE
RISING TO HIS FALL
GOD, HE WAS SO YOUNG
LIKE A SONG HALF SUNG
INTERRUPTED BY
SOMEONE JUST AS SHY
WHO NEVER KNEW HIS NAME
THE TRUE COST OF HONOR
IS SUDDENLY TOO CLEAR
IN MEASURES TOO FULL AND DEAR
HE ALWAYS LOOKS THE SAME
DRESSED IN BLUE OR GRAY
ALL THE LIFE HE'LL MISS
GIRLS HE'LL NEVER KISS
THINGS HE'LL NEVER TRY
UNAWARE THAT I
NEVER KNEW HIS NAME
I NEVER KNEW HIS NAME
GUESS IT'S JUST AS WELL
SO I DO MY PART
HIDING FROM MY HEART
WHISPERING GOOD-BYE
THANKING GOD THAT I
NEVER KNEW HIS NAME

12 REGIMENTAL DRUMMER

MICHAEL ENGLISH

A war-weary Confederate soldier draws the strength to carry on from the memory of his regiment's fallen drummer boy.

HE RAN OFF TO FIND ADVENTURE
AT THE TENDER AGE OF NINE
LIKE SO MANY OTHER SONS OF OLD VIRGINIA
AND THOUGH HE WAS TOO SMALL TO HOLD A RIFLE
HE WOULD BANG A DRUM AND SMILE
AS A REGIMENTAL DRUMMER FOR A WHILE
WITH A HEART AS GREEN AS SUMMER
AND A LAUGH AS RICH AS GOLD
HE WOULD POLISH UP THE OLD DREAMS
SO LONG FORGOTTEN
BUT SOMEWHERE ON THE ROAD
BACK HOME FROM SHILOH
HE GOT OLDER THAN HIS YEARS
AS THE REGIMENTAL DRUMMER CRIED OUR TEARS
AND IN HIS EYES I'D SOMETIMES SEE
THE BOY THAT I USED TO BE
AND FOR A MOMENT I COULD LEAVE
THIS ALL BEHIND
THEN ALL AT ONCE THE BOY WAS GONE
LOST ON THIS ROAD WE'RE ON
JUST ANOTHER FALLEN BROTHER
I STILL THINK OF HIM EACH MORNING
AND I PRAY FOR HIM EACH NIGHT
JUST A REGIMENTAL DRUMMER
FOR OLD VIRGINIA
AND WHEN I CLOSE MY EYES I STILL REMEMBER
HOW HE'D BANG HIS DRUM AND SMILE
SO I MARCH A LITTLE FARTHER
WHEN I HEAR THE DRUMMER'S CALL
FOR THE REGIMENTAL DRUMMER IN US ALL
THE INNOCENCE IN ME HAS DIED
LOST SOMEWHERE DEEP INSIDE
LIKE ANOTHER FALLEN BROTHER
DOWN THE DUSTY ROADS BEHIND ME
TO THE ONES STILL UP AHEAD
THERE'S A REGIMENTAL DRUMMER
FROM OLD VIRGINIA
WHO WILL ALWAYS FALL IN STEP BESIDE ME
AND BANG HIS DRUM AND SMILE
SO I MARCH A LITTLE FARTHER
WHEN I HEAR THE LONG ROLL START
FOR THE REGIMENTAL DRUMMER IN MY HEART

13 THE HONOR OF YOUR NAME

TRISHA YEARWOOD

The young wife we met in "Missing You (My Bill)" learns of her husband's death and writes him one last letter.

TODAY A MAN CAME TO OUR DOOR
DRESSED IN BLACK WITH NEWS OF WAR
A FACE I'VE NEVER SEEN BEFORE
BUT, BILL, I NEVER WILL FORGET HIM
I KNEW AT ONCE THAT YOU WERE GONE
HE TIPPED HIS HAT AND THEN MOVED ON
AND LEFT MY WORLD A COLD AND EMPTY SPACE
SUCH A LONELY PLACE
BUT FOR THE PROMISE
THAT WE MADE SO LONG AGO
FOR THE NIGHTS
WHEN YOU HELD ME IN YOUR ARMS
I WILL KEEP LIFE'S FRAGILE FLAME
FOR THE HONOR OF YOUR NAME
I DON'T KNOW WHAT TO DO RIGHT NOW
EXCEPT TO STRUGGLE ON SOMEHOW
I'VE LEARNED TO SOW, I'LL LEARN TO PLOW
AND, BILL, I NEVER WILL FORGET YOU
THE KIDS AND I MIGHT MOVE OUT WEST
I'LL TAKE OUR DREAM AND LEAVE THE REST
THERE'S NOTHIN' FOR MY BROKEN HEART TO DO
'CEPT WRITE THESE WORDS TO YOU
FOR THE PROMISE
THAT WE MADE SO LONG AGO
FOR THE LOVE
ALL THE LOVE THAT WILL NOT DIE
I WILL KEEP LIFE'S FRAGILE FLAME
FOR THE HONOR OF YOUR NAME
AND MAYBE SOMEDAY WHEN I'M STRONGER
I WILL LOOK BACK ON THIS DAY
AND UNDERSTAND ALL THE REASONS WHY
THE GOOD LORD TOOK YOU AWAY
BUT FOR THE PROMISE
THAT WE MADE SO LONG AGO
FOR THE MAN
THAT I SEE IN OUR SON'S EYES
I WILL KEEP LIFE'S FRAGILE FLAME
FOR THE HONOR OF YOUR NAME

14 IN GREAT DEEDS

CHARLIE DANIELS

In great deeds something abides.
On great fields, something stays.
Forms change and pass, bodies disappear
But spirits linger
To consecrate ground for the vision-place of the Soul.
And reverent men and women from afar
And generations that know us not and that we know not of,
Shall come here to ponder and to dream
And the power of the vision shall pass into their souls.

-Joshua Lawrence Chamberlain

15 LAST WALTZ FOR DIXIE

JOHN BERRY

Our "Virginia" Captain exhorts his men to do the undoable on the eve of the Battle of Gettysburg.

HERE TONIGHT ...
AS I LOOK UPON THE FACES OF MY BROTHERS
I REMEMBER ALL THE OTHERS WHO ARE GONE
SAFE IN HIS GRACE
WATCHING OVER THIS PLACE
WITH THE DAWN ...
INTO HIS HANDS WE SHALL SURRENDER
TO HIS GLORY
AND WHEN THEY TELL THE STORY LET THEM SAY
OF THE SONS OF THE GRAY
NOT ONE TURNED AWAY
IT'S THE LAST WALTZ FOR DIXIE
IT'S THE LAST SONG SHE'LL SING
SO PLAY IT WITH PRIDE
FOR ALL THOSE WHO DIED
AND THE SPIRIT INSIDE YOU
THAT'S THE DIXIE IN ME
I BELIEVE ...
THERE HAS NEVER BEEN
A GROUP OF MEN SO SPLENDID
OR A CAUSE SO WELL-DEFENDED AS OUR OWN
BE IT HEAVEN OR HELL
HAIL AND FAREWELL
IT'S THE LAST WALTZ FOR DIXIE
IT'S THE LAST SONG SHE'LL SING
SO PLAY IT WITH PRIDE
FOR ALL THOSE WHO DIED
AND THE SPIRIT INSIDE YOU
THAT'S THE DIXIE IN ME
FOR ALL WE HOLD DEAR
THE ROAD AHEAD IS CLEAR
FOR ALL THE THINGS WE HONOR
THE MOMENT IS HERE
IT'S THE LAST WALTZ FOR DIXIE
IT'S THE LAST SONG SHE'LL SING
SO PLAY IT WITH PRIDE
FOR ALL THOSE WHO DIED
AND THE SPIRIT INSIDE YOU
THAT'S THE DIXIE IN ME

The Authors

Photo: Beth Kelly

FRANK WILDHORN (Author, Composer) With *Jekyll & Hyde* (celebrating its second smash year) at the Plymouth Theatre and *The Scarlet Pimpernel* running at the Minskoff Theater, Mr. Wildhorn is the only American composer with two original shows running simultaneously on Broadway. Mr. Wildhorn also wrote songs for *Victor/Victoria* on Broadway as well as original music for Arthur Kopit's *Road to Nirvana, Cyrano* and *Svengali* (Alley Theatre). Among the artists who have recorded and performed Mr. Wildhorn's music are Whitney Houston, Julie Andrews, Sammy Davis, Jr., Liza Minelli, Kenny Rogers, Trisha Yearwood, Natalie Cole, The Moody Blues, Jennifer Holliday, Ben Vereen, Peabo Bryson, BeBe & CeCe Winans, Molly Hatchet, Hootie & the Blowfish, Deana Carter, Travis Tritt, Tracy Lawrence, Amy Grant, Freddie Jackson, Brenda Russell, John Raitt, Regina Bell, Patti LaBelle, Anthony Warlow, Colm Wilkinson and Linda Eder Wildhorn, whose Atlantic debut album *It's Time* he co-produced. In development are *Havana* (Gregory Boyd, Jack Murphy, Jerry Zaks), *Alice Vampyr, Big Nose* and *Pirate Girls.* Mr. Wildhorn is the creative director of Atlantic Theatre/Atlantic Records and is associate artist of the Alley Theatre.

Photo: Beth Kelly

JACK MURPHY has worked on a wide variety of projects as both lyricist and composer. Collaborating with Frank Wildhorn, he wrote lyrics for Linda Eder's EMI album *And So Much More,* as well as ten songs on her latest Atlantic album *It's Time.* In collaboration with Mary Bracken Phillips, he composed the score for the musical *Silver Dollar,* which debuted last year at the Goodspeed Opera House, with a second production at the State One Theater in Wichita. He has written and performed albums for many record labels including A&M, Verve, MGM, Elektra, Columbia and ABC Dunhill, and was staff writer for United Artists Music. For television, he has composed music ranging from dance segments for the "Sesame Street" Muppets to lyrics for the title song of the ABC Movie of the Week *Lies of the Heart.* Most recently, again in collaboration with Frank Wildhorn and Gregory Boyd of the Alley Theatre in Houston, Texas, he has written the lyrics for *The Civil War Part One - An American Musical,* a double CD which will be released on Atlantic Records in October of 1998 featuring Betty Buckley, Linda Eder, Carl Anderson, Michel Belle, Trisha Yearwood, Tracy Lawrence, Deana Carter, Kevin Sharp, Hootie & the Blowfish, Dr. John, Travis Tritt, Trace Adkins and many more. Mr. Murphy is currently working on (again with collaborators Frank Wildhorn and Gregory Boyd) two new musicals, *Havana,* scheduled to be workshopped this spring, and *Alice,* an *Alice in Wonderland* for the '90s . Mr. Murphy is published by Cherry Lane Music Publishing in New York.

GREGORY BOYD became the artistic director of the Alley Theatre in 1989. During his tenure, the Alley has risen to national and international prominence, winning the 1996 Tony Award, while also creating productions that have moved to Broadway, major European festivals (including an unprecedented two in one season at the Venice Biennale) and on record-setting tours to forty American cities, as well as in London, Paris and Berlin. Mr. Boyd has directed more than twenty Alley productions, including Frank Wildhorn's *Jekyll & Hyde* (premiere) and *Svengali* (premiere), which he also co-authored. He directed the recording of *Jekyll & Hyde* (for Atlantic Records) and supervised the premiere of *The Civil War* (which he co-wrote with Frank Wildhorn and Jack Murphy). He has served as panelist for the National Endowment of the Arts, the Texas Commission on the Arts, and the Massachusetts Council for the Arts. He has directed theatre and opera across America, including eleven seasons at the Williamstown Theatre Festival as director and actor, and has taught on the faculties of Carnegie Mellon, Williams College and the University of North Carolina, where he headed the Professional Theatre Training Program.

Photo: Jim Caldwell

CONTENTS

PROLOGUE

Text by
JACK MURPHY and GREGORY BOYD

Music by
FRANK WILDHORN

Monologue:
On the twelfth of April, 1861, Confederate guns opened fire on Fort Sumter in Charleston Harbor, thus beginning the bloodiest conflict in American history. Six hundred twenty thousand casualties; more than all other American wars combined. The Civil War remains this nation's single most defining experience, ultimately giving new meaning to the word freedom. Walt Whitman, a young newspaperman destined to become America's greatest poet, wrote, "Future years will never know the seething hell and the black infernal background of this war. And it is best they should not. The real war will never get into the books."

THE DAY THE SUN STOOD STILL

Lyrics by
JACK MURPHY

Music by
FRANK WILDHORN

*Recorded a half step higher.

G
Em
hell and pur - ga - to - ry to the boys who wore the blue. And I
guns rolled out like thun - der, and the black smoke burned my eyes. And I
prayed for night to save us, and I cried and bowed my head. But the
F
G/B
E
Am
thought I'd seen it all till the day night would n't fall. Oh, how the
watched it all un - fold just the way the Bi - ble told Josh - u - a's
sun just kept a - creep - in' 'cross a cold, in - dif - f'rent sky, cast - in' a
1.
F
G
sun did blaze, would-n't go down for days. 2. I got
end less day, keep - in' the
dead - ly glow on all the

2.3.
G
Am
night at bay. And the sol - diers kept a - com - in' till the
men be - low. All the ho - urs in a life - time don't add
F
G
ground looked like a sea of blue and gray. And I
up to one whole min - ute in that sun. And the
Am
F
watched them from a dis - tance, won-d'rin'. if I would-'ve fought or run a - way.
he - roes and the cow - ards look the same when they have fal - len by the gun.
G
Chorus:
C
The day the sun stood still, how they beat the blood - y drums,
The day the sun stood still, and the North and South looked west,
cresc.
f

G
Am
and the sec-onds moved like ho - urs, but the sun - set nev - er comes.
but the eve-ning star was sleep - in', and the day - light would - n't rest.
F
C
And the can-nons shake the ground, and the bul-lets test your will.
Out on the kill - ing floor, the red sun on the hill
G
Am
E - ven shad-ows find no cov - er on that God - for - sak - en hill,
shin - in' down on all the dead men with a strange and ee - rie chill,
1.
D.S. 𝄋
F
G
C5
F2
the day the sun stood still.
3. And I
dim.
mf

2.
F G F/C C
the day the sun stood still.
Bridge:
B♭ F
Do not judge what your broth - er does
C G
till you've walked a mile, rank by blood - y file.
B♭ F
Who's to say if you run or stay and fight?

G
The day the sun stood still
Chorus:
C
G
is just beneath the skin in the soul of ev-'ry sol-
How they'll beat the blood-y drums! And the sec-onds move like ho-
Am
F
dier, ev-'ry bat-tle that he's in. The day the sun stood still
urs, but the sun-set nev-er comes. And the can-nons shake the ground,
C
G
will haunt your dreams at night and stalk you ev-'ry sun-
and the bul-lets test your will. E-ven shad-ows find no cov-

1.
2.
Am
F
G
C2
F2
N.C.
C
rise, though you will not know - it till ___ the day the sun _ stands still. _
er on some God-for - sak - en hill, _
___ the day the sun _ stood still,
dim.
mf
the day the sun _ stood still, ___
the day the sun ___ stood still.
rit. e dim.
mp

MISSING YOU (MY BILL)

Lyrics by
JACK MURPHY

Music by
FRANK WILDHORN

G Bm
B♭ Dm
And Bil - ly helped and scraped his knee,
You al - ways meant to get to it,
C G/D D B
E♭ B♭/F F D
but he took it all in stride.
but I know you had to leave.
Em G7 C F7(♭5)
Gm B♭7 E♭ A♭7(♭5)
Day by day I get by, mak - ing do the best I can.
Thank God there's so much to do. It's the work that gets me through.
Chorus:
C/D D G C
E♭/F F B♭ E♭
When the sun slow - ly sets just be - hind
mf

D/F♯ G C D/F♯
F/A B♭ E♭ F/A
our hill, then the mem - o - ries come in the eve -
G C
B♭ E♭
ning chill. How I long for your touch like a
D/F♯ Em Cmaj7
F/A Gm E♭maj7
lov - er will! Oh, I'm miss - ing you. God, I'm
C/D D Cmaj9 D/C Cmaj9 D/C C/D
E♭/F F E♭maj9 F/E♭ E♭maj9 F/E♭ E♭/F
1.
miss-ing you, my Bill.

2.
Bridge:
G F C/E
B♭ A♭ E♭/G
So I count the days, and I think of ways to
G D/G G Gsus G
B♭ F/B♭ B♭ B♭sus B♭
speed them by.
When the
F C/E
A♭ E♭/G
day is through, I re - mem - ber you and cry.
C/D D
E♭/F F
When the

Chorus:
G C D/F♯ G C D/F♯
B♭ E♭ F/A B♭ E♭ F/A
sun slow-ly sets just be-hind our hill, then the mem-o-ries come in the eve-
G C D/F♯ Em
B♭ E♭ F/A Gm
ning chill. How I long for your touch like a lov-er will! Oh, I'm
mp
Cmaj7 C/D D
E♭maj7 E♭/F F N.C.
miss-ing you. God, I'm miss-ing you, my Bill.
Cmaj9 D/C Cmaj9 D/C D7sus G
E♭maj9 F/E♭ E♭maj9 F/E♭ F7sus B♭
rit.

VIRGINIA

Lyrics by
JACK MURPHY

Music by
FRANK WILDHORN

D(9) A C♯m7 Bm7 C♯m7 G D/E
pleas - ure the eyes, where the old was new and the fool - ish wise. I can
all of your sons who will stand and fall 'neath the cease - less guns.
Chorus:
D A E/G♯ A D A/C♯
hear Vir-gin - ia when the south wind sings, and I see her shin-ing on a
D Esus D A C♯7 F♯m
black-bird's sil-ver wings. And I can feel Vir-gin - ia run-ning through my soul, when the
To Coda
1.
D(9) Esus Bm/A A Bm/A A
flag un-furls and the drum-mers start their long, long roll.
2. Oh, sa - cred

2.
N.C.
A
E/D
D
C♯m7
Bm7
Will I ev - er see her rise a - gain, or are the old days gone? Has the
C♯m7
Esus
E
A
world moved on?
Will she ev - er grace our
3
E/D
D
C♯m7
E6
D.S. 𝄋 al Coda
eyes a - gain? Tell me when? I can
rit.
a tempo
Coda
Bm/D
A
E/G♯
A
roll. Oh, Vir - gin -

D A/C♯ D E D A
ia. I can feel Vir-gin - ia run-ning
C♯7 F♯m D(9) Esus
through my soul, when the flag un - furls and the drum-mers start their
Bm/A A D(9) A/C♯ Bm7 Bm/A A
freely
long, long roll. When the flag un - furls and the drum-mers start their long, long roll.
rit.
freely
E/A Dmaj7 A E/A Dmaj7 A(9)
a tempo

OLD GRAY COAT

Lyrics by
JACK MURPHY

Music by
FRANK WILDHORN

C G A7 D
twen-ty shades of gray, and the waist is shrunk too tight. And the
B7 Em B7 Em7
bot-tom's caked and mud-dy, and the but-tons are half gone. But
Moderately fast country rock ♩ = 144
Am7 G/B C A7/C♯ D5
just like you and me, this old gray coat wears on. And when I die
Chorus:
G B7 Em
in this gray coat,
1.3. I'm gon-na march through heav-en's door.
2. and when they come to bur-y me,

A
Am
I'm gon - na walk up to Saint
if they com - mence to speech - a -
G/B
C
Pe - ter and tell him, "Send me back for more."
fy - in' and sing - in' "Near - er Lord to Thee,"
D
G
'Cause I'll be damned if I'll just
well, be damn sure I ain't just
B7
Em
sit a - round, while you boys win the war.
sleep - in' 'cause I flat out guar - an - tee

A
N.C.
G
B7
'Cause e - ven when I'm
that e - ven when I'm
Em
N.C.
G
B7
dead, shot full of yan - kee
dead, shot full of yan - kee
Em
Am
G/B
lead,
lead,
1. there'll be part of me, keeps
2. that the tough - est part lives
3. there ain't noth - in' that I'd
C
A/C#
D5
hang - ing by a thread
on in ev - 'ry shred
rath - er wear in - stead

N.C.
G
To Coda II
C9
of this old gray coat.
G
To Coda I
C9
Verse 2:
G
2.When I think of all the
C
G
plac - es this old coat and me have been, through the
C
G
A
fat and lean and in be - tween, dou - ble quick through thick and thin,

D G
from the ball - rooms down in Rich - mond, to the
C G C
top of Mar - ye's Heights, from Ma - nas - sas to The
G A D
Wil - der - ness, and a hun - dred oth - er fights. Now, the
B Em B
col - lar's torn and tat - tered, and the el - bow's worn clean

Em
Am
G/B
C
A/C♯
through. But bud - dy, in a pinch, this old gray coat
D
D.S. 𝄋 al Coda I
will do. And when I die
Coda
C9
Well, you can
Bridge:
N.C.
B
B/D♯
Em
B
B/F♯
cut my throat. You can sink my boat.
bones you tote, when that's all she wrote,
Em
Am
G/B
C
A/C♯
But you can nev - er stop this old gray coat.
I'll fight on in - side this old gray coat.

D
1.
2.
D.S. 𝄋 al Coda II
When my
'Cause when I die
Coda II
C9
G
C9
This old gray coat.
I'll go down
G
C7
G
in this old gray coat,
C7
B♭5
F5
C5
G5
in this old gray coat.

I'LL NEVER PASS THIS WAY AGAIN

Lyrics by
JACK MURPHY

Music by
FRANK WILDHORN

I'll Never Pass This Way Again - 5 - 1
0306B

G
Em
But I nev - er seemed to no - tice that the
But I nev - er heard the se - crets that she
And if I had a pen - ny, I would
Am7
D
G
wa - ter ran this clear. And I've nev - er seen that
whis - pers on the breeze. For the on - ly sound on
wish me a spell. I would kneel, and pray that
To Coda
B7
Em
A7
col - or green spar - kle down the glen. Now, I'll
hal-lowed ground is the si - lence of the men who will
here I'd stay for -

Am7 G/B C C/D G
nev - er pass this way a - gain.
nev - er pass this way a - gain.
1. 2. Bridge:
Gsus/A G/B C
2. I have It nev - er shone as
G/B Am D7 G
beau - ti - ful as how it looks to - day. We
Em A7 Am
nev - er miss the things we love till they go a - way.

D C G/B
But I have heard the bu - gler's call, and it's
B7 Em G/A A
time for me to leave, 'cause there comes a day when a
G/A A Am7 C/D
D.S. al Coda
man must say "I will die for what I be - lieve." 3. I have
Coda
Em A7
ev - er, a - men. But I'll
rit.
a tempo

Am7 G/B C C/D Am7 G/B C
never pass this way, no, I'll nev - er pass this way,
C/D Am7 G/B C(9)
no, I'll nev - er pass this way,
Freely
N.C.
G
a - gain.
C G
rit.

RIVER JORDAN

Lyrics by
JACK MURPHY

Music by
FRANK WILDHORN

Db Ab/C Bbm7 Ab/C Db Ab/C Bb7
lev - y, till we lay our bur - dens down and
Bbm7/Eb Eb7 Ab D7(b5 b9)
die. But they say there's a new wind
Db Ab/C Bbm7 Ab/C Db Bb7/D Bbm7/Eb
blow - in' down by the might-y Mis-sis-sip - pi dressed in
Ab Bbm7 Bbm7/Eb Ebm7/Ab D7(#9) Db Ab/C Bbm7 Ab/C Db
blue. Shak-in' loose these chains that bind me till this

B♭m7 A♭/C B♭7/D B♭m7/E♭
end - less night is fi - nal - ly through. So
Chorus:
A♭ D♭ A♭/C B♭m7
meet me by the riv - er Jor - dan,
B♭m7/E♭ A♭ B♭m7 B♭m7/E♭
knee deep in a ris - ing tide. We will
A♭7 D7(♭5 ♭9) D♭ B♭m7
climb a - board that boat called free - dom, and we'll

B♭7
B♭m7/E♭
all sail o - ver to the oth - er side.
E♭
C7/E
Fm
A♭7
A♭7/C
D♭
Sail on, just sail, sail on,
B♭m7
A♭/C
B♭7/D
B♭m7/E♭
sail on o - ver to the oth - er side.
E♭
C7/E
Fm
A♭7
A♭7/C
D♭
Sail, sail on, just sail on, just

Bbm7 Ab/C Db Bbm7/Eb Db/Ab Ab
sail on o - ver to the oth - er side. So
Fast ♩ = 132
Db Ab/C Db Bb7/D
meet me by the riv - er Jor - dan,
Bbm7/Eb Ab
knee deep in the ris - ing tide. We'll
Ab7 Db Ab Bbm7 Ab Bbm7
climb a - board that boat called free - dom, and we'll

Ab/C Db Bbm7/Eb Db/Ab Ab
all sail on o - ver to the oth - er side, where we'll be
Db Ab Bbm7 Ab/C Db Bb7/D
sing - in' hal - le - lu - jah when this
Bbm7/Eb Ab
mis - er - y sure 'nough be past. We'll be
Ab7 Db Ab Bbm7 Ab Bbm7
sing - ing hal - le - lu - jah. Hal - le -

Ab/C
Db
Bbm7/Eb
Db/Ab
Ab
lu - jah, we are now free at last. You got to
Eb
C7/E
Fm
Ab
Db
hold on, hold on when
Bbm7
Ab/C
Bbm7/Eb
C7/E
Fm
you live east of E - den, you got to pray that you'll
Bb7
Bbm7/Eb
find your-self in par - a - dise some day. So just

Ab
Db
Bbm7 Ab/C Db Bb7/D
meet me by the riv - er Jor - dan,
Bbm7/Eb
Ab
knee deep in a ris - in' tide. We'll
Ab7
Db Ab Bbm7 Ab Bbm7
climb a - board that boat called free - dom, and we'll
Ab/C Db Bbm7/Eb Db/Ab Ab
all sail on o - ver to the oth - er side.

A♭7
D♭7
A♭7
D♭7
A♭7
D♭7
A♭7
D♭7
B♭7
E♭7
B♭7
E♭7
B♭7
E♭7
B♭7
E♭7
So

B♭ E♭ B♭/D E♭ C7/E
meet me by the riv - er Jor - dan,
Cm7/F B♭
knee deep in the ris - ing tide. We'll
B♭7 E♭ B♭ Cm7 B♭ Cm7
climb a - board that boat called free - dom, and we'll
B♭/D E♭ Cm7/F E♭/B♭ B♭
all sail on o - ver to the oth - er side, where we'll be

E♭ B♭ Cm7 B♭/D E♭ C7/E
sing - in' hal - le - lu - jah when this
Cm7/F B♭
mis - er - y sure 'nough be past. We'll be
B♭7 E♭ B♭ Cm7 B♭ Cm7
sing - ing hal - le - lu - jah. Hal - le -
B♭/D E♭ Cm7/F E♭/B♭ B♭
lu - jah, we are now free at last. You got to

F D7/F♯ Gm B♭ E♭
hold on, hold on when
Cm7 B♭/D Cm7/F D7/F♯ Gm
you live east of E - den, you got to pray that you'll
C7 Cm7/F
find your - self in par - a - dise some day. So just
B♭ E♭ Cm7 B♭/D E♭ C7/E
meet me by the riv - er Jor - dan,

Cm7/F
B♭
knee deep in a ris - in' tide. We'll
B♭7
E♭
B♭
Cm7
B♭/D
E♭
climb a - board that boat called free - dom, and we'll
Cm7
B♭/D
E♭
Cm7/F
B♭7
freely
all sail right on o - ver to the oth - er side.
B♭7
E♭7
B♭7
E♭7
Repeat ad lib. and fade
Hal - le - lu - jah! Hal - le - lu - jah!
a tempo

WITH THESE HANDS

Lyrics by
JACK MURPHY

Music by
FRANK WILDHORN

A/C♯ E/G♯ Bsus B
feel of you at sun - down, run - nin'
A/C♯ E/G♯ Bsus B
fi - re through my veins.
Verses 2 & 3:
G D/G
(She:) 2. Look at these hands, they've been hold - in' on and pray - ing, and they're
(He:) 3. Look at these eyes, they have seen so man - y dev - ils. They can
C/G B7sus B
trem - bling for your qui - et, eas - y touch. Look at these
hard - ly rec - og - nize the an - gel here. (She:) I on - ly

Em
G/D
C
3
hands reach - ing out for the man I love too
know when I look in your eyes, you calm all my
Dsus
D
B♭maj7
much.
fears.
(He:) Come to me now, whis - per
(He:) We've got to - night, dar - lin'
E♭maj9
Am7
se - crets soft and low.
we can't ask for more.
(She:) Lay here be - side me, dar - lin',
(She:) Just hold me tight, leave the
1.
To Next Strain
Am7/D
F♯m7/B
don't let me go.
(He:) With these hands,

2.
Am7/D
F♯m7/B
Chorus:
E
(Both:)
E/G♯
world out - side the door.
(He:) With these eyes.
I could hold you
I could see you
for -
A
F♯m
B7
E
ev - er.
With this heart, I will al - ways be true.
(She:) Just like
(She:) Like the
A
E/G♯
G♯
C♯m
B
A
F♯m7/B
God in his heav - en, (He:) may you al - ways be there (Both:) ev-'ry time that these hands reach for
stars in the heav - ens, (He:) my love will be there (Both:) ev-'ry time that these eyes look at
1.
A/E
E
A/E
E
Am7/D
2.
A/E
E
you.
you.

Bridge:
E/G♯ A B/D♯ E E/G♯ A
(He:)
(She:) With these hands, (He:) with these eyes, (Both:) with this heart, I'll be there.
D F♯m7/B Gm7/C
(She:) I'll be there.
(He:) With these hands,
Chorus:
F F/A B♭ Gm C7
(Both:)
I could hold you for-ev-er. With this heart, I will al-ways be
F B♭ F/A A Dm C
(He:)
true. (She:) Just like God in his heav-en, may you al-ways be there (Both:) ev-'ry

B♭ Gm7/C F F/A Dm7 B♭ F/A
(He:)
time that these hands reach for you. (She:) Just like God in his heav - en, my
A Dm C B♭ Gm7/C
love will be there, (Both:) ev - 'ry time that these hands reach for
B♭/F F B♭ Gm7/C B♭ F/A
Freely
(He:)
you. (She:) Ev-'ry time that these hands reach for you.
rit.
a tempo
A Dm C B♭ F
rit.

JUDGMENT DAY

Lyrics by
JACK MURPHY

Music by
FRANK WILDHORN

Guitar→ (capo 4th fret)
Piano→
Am G Am G Am G/A
C♯m B C♯m B C♯m B/C♯
mf
Am G/A Am G/A Am G/A
C♯m B/C♯ C♯m B/C♯ C♯m B/C♯
Verse:
Am G Am G
C♯m B C♯m B
1. I sit a - mong my charts and maps and hear the lone - ly call of taps
2. I write to moth - ers of their sons and say they were the brav - est ones.
C Am G/A
E C♯m B/C♯
like the wind a - cross the moon.
Then I pour a drink and sleep.

Am G Am G
C♯m B C♯m B
I pray to God_ that I___ am right___ and then I send_ boys off___ to fight___
But sleep is on - ly filled_ with drums,_ a slice of death_ till morn - ing comes,__
C Am
E C♯m
___ and trav - el home_ in box - es far too___ soon.___ May
___ the heart of dark - nes where_ my soul can___ weep.___ Come
D C G D7/F♯ Em
F♯ E B F♯7/A♯ G♯m
(1. 3.) God have mer - cy on___ my soul_ for all the years_ that I___ have sto - len
(2.) walk a mile_ in blood - y shoes_ and lose the men_ that I___ am los - ing.

D C Em
F♯ E G♯m
from the men who fol - low what I say. And
Watch them pay the pip - er for my tune. Come
D C G D7/F♯ Em
F♯ E B F♯7/A♯ G♯m
may their fam - 'lies all for - give the or - ders I so calm - ly give them,
walk a - mong their ghosts with me and look through eyes too used to see - ing
D C D
F♯ E F♯
as I march their sons in - to harm's way. (1. 3.) And
fac - es who have joined the lost pla - toon. (2.) Come
Chorus: G F C G/B Am
B A E B/D♯ C♯m
out there on the kill - ing floor, I hear the blood - y sounds of war and
Judg - ment Day, God on - ly knows if man will reap the pain he sows and

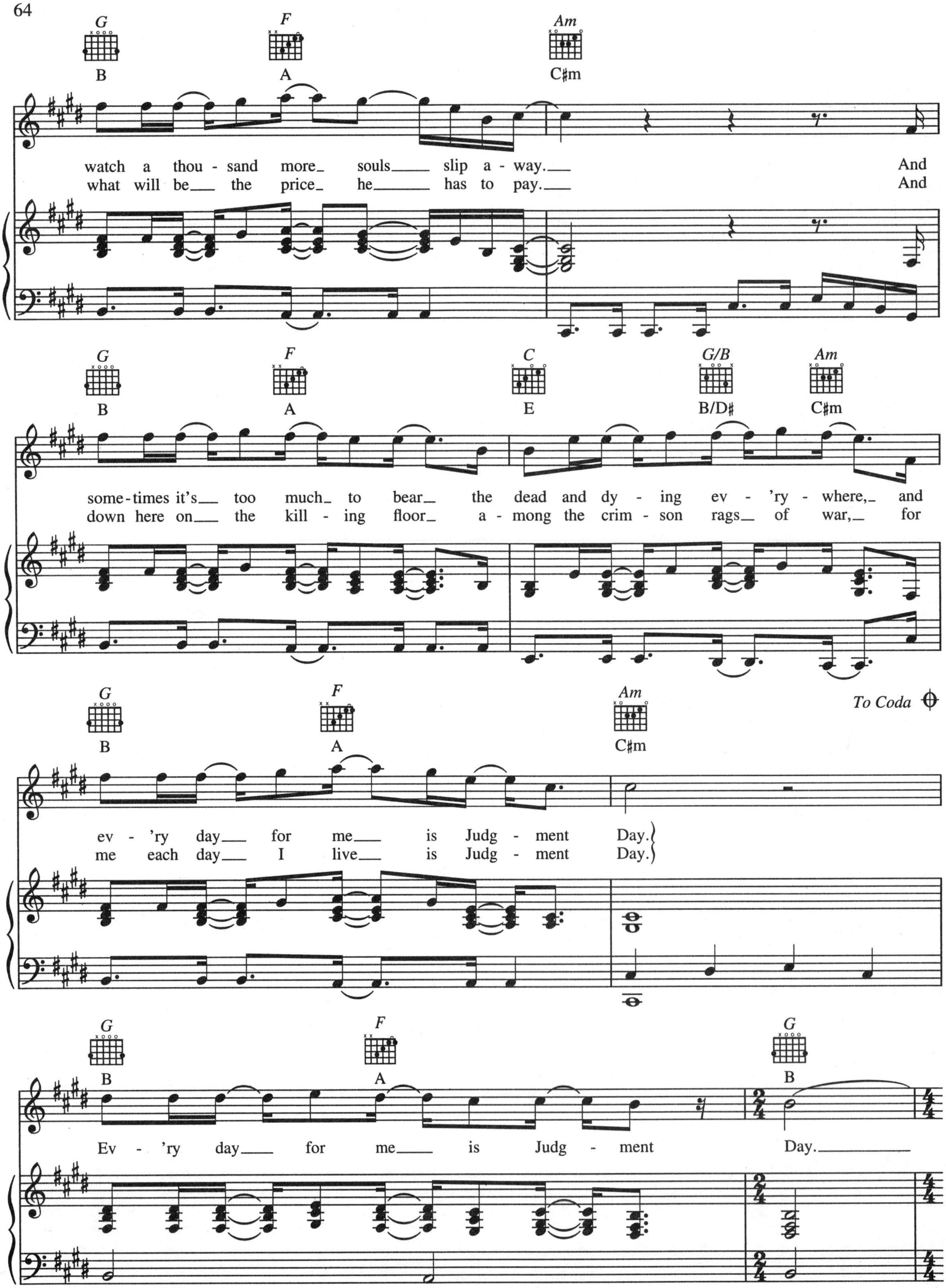
G F Am
B A C♯m
watch a thou - sand more souls slip a - way. And
what will be the price he has to pay. And
G F C G/B Am
B A E B/D♯ C♯m
some - times it's too much to bear the dead and dy - ing ev - 'ry - where, and
down here on the kill - ing floor a - mong the crim - son rags of war, for
G F Am
B A C♯m
To Coda
ev - 'ry day for me is Judg - ment Day.
me each day I live is Judg - ment Day.
G F G
B A B
Ev - 'ry day for me is Judg - ment Day.

1.
Am
C♯m
2.
Am
C♯m
Am
G
Am
G
C♯m
B
C♯m
B
1.
F
G
Am
A
B
C♯m
2.
F
G
A
B

Am
C♯m
G
B
Am
C♯m
G
B
F
A
G
B
Am
C♯m
D.S. 𝄋 al Coda
May
Coda
G
B
F
A
Am
C♯m
Ev - 'ry day for me is Judg - ment Day, ev - 'ry day.
G
B
F
A
G
B
Am
C♯m
Ev - 'ry day for me is Judg - ment Day.
rit.

TELL MY FATHER

Lyrics by
JACK MURPHY

Music by
FRANK WILDHORN

G G7 Csus C G
tried to re - mem - ber you are judged by what you do
truth could grow old - er. Tell my fa - ther when you can,
D C 1. G D 2. G D/F♯
while pass-ing through.
I was a man.
Bridge:
Em D/F♯ G G7 C
Tell him we will meet a - gain, where the an - gels learn to
(instrumental solo ad lib. . . .
D Em D/F♯ G G7
fly. Tell him we will meet as men, for, with

C
Dsus
D
G
hon - or, did I ___ die.
. . . end solo)
Tell him how I wore the
Tell him how I wore the
Dsus
D
G
G7
Csus
C
Blue proud and ___ true through the fi - re.
Blue proud and ___ true like he taught ___ me.
G
1.
D
C/G
C/E
D/F♯
Tell my fa - ther ___ so he'll know I love him so.
Tell my fa - ther ___ not to
G
D/F♯
2.
Dsus
D
Freely
C/G
G
cry, then say "good - bye."
rit.

I NEVER KNEW HIS NAME

Lyrics by
JACK MURPHY

Music by
FRANK WILDHORN

Em E Am D7/F♯
wise, try - ing not to cry. Now he's gone and
sung, in - ter - rup - ted __ by some - one just as
Dm7 F/G 1. C F
I nev - er knew his name.
shy who nev - er knew his
2. C F/C C Bridge: F/A E7
name. The true cost of hon - or is
cresc.
mf
Am C7 G/F Bm7(♭5)
sud - den - ly too clear in meas - ures too full and
rall. decresc.

Em
Gsus
G
dear.
a tempo
rit.
Verse:
C
Bm7(♭5)
E7
He always looks the same, dressed in blue or
a tempo
mp
Am
G
Fmaj7
G/F
gray. All the life he'll miss, girls he'll nev - er
Em7
E
Am
D7/F♯
kiss, things he'll nev - er try, un - a - ware that

Instrumental:
Dm7 F/G C
I nev - er knew his name.
mf
Bm7(♭5) E7(♭9) Am G
F G/F F F/G G F/G G Am/G G7
cresc.
rit.
C Bm7(♭5) E7(♭9)
I nev - er knew his name. Guess it's just as
a tempo
f
mf

Am
G
Fmaj7
G/F
well, so I do my part hid - ing from my
Em
E7
Am
heart, whis - per - ing good - bye,
dim.
mp
D7/F♯
Dm7
F/G
C
thank-ing God that I nev - er knew his name.
rit. e dim.
a tempo
p
Fm6
C2
rit.
molto rit.

REGIMENTAL DRUMMER

Lyrics by
JACK MURPHY

Music by
FRANK WILDHORN

Csus C B♭ A
- ia. Though he was too small to hold a ri - fle, he would
- ten. But some-where on the road back home from Shi - loh, he got
Dm F7 B♭ C
bang his drum and smile as the reg - i - men - tal drum - mer for a while.
old - er than his years as the reg - i - men - tal drum - mer cried our tears.
1. 2.
B♭ F/A Gm F B♭ F/A Gm F
2. With a
cresc.

Chorus:
F/C Bb F/C C A/C#
And in his eyes, I'd some-times see the boy that I used to be. For a
mf
Dm G7 Csus C
mo-ment, I could leave this all be-hind.
F Bb F/C C A/C#
Then, all at once, the boy was gone, lost on the road we're on, just an-
Dm G7 Csus C
oth-er fall-en broth-er. I still
dim.

Verse 3:
F Bb F
think of him each morning, and I pray for him each night. Just a
mp
Dm G7 Csus C
reg - i - men - tal drum - mer for old Vir-gin - ia. And when I close my
Bb A Dm F7 F7/A
eyes, I still re - mem-ber how he'd bang his drum and smile. So, I
Bb F/A A7sus A7 Dm F7/C
march a lit - tle far - ther when I hear the drum-mer's call for the

B♭
C
B♭
F/A
Gm
reg - i - men - tal drum - mer in us all.
cresc.
F
B♭/F
F
B♭/F
B♭/C
mf
F
B♭/F
E♭
Csus
F/C
Csus
F/C
C
A/C♯
The in - no-cence in me has died,
lost some-where deep in - side like an -

Dm G7 Csus C
oth - er fall - en broth - er. 4. Down the
mp
Verse 4:
F B♭ F
dust - y roads be - hind me, to the ones still up a - head, there's a
Dm G7 Csus C
reg - i - men - tal drum - mer from old Vir - gin - ia who will al - ways
B♭ A Dm F7
fall in step be - side me and bang his drum and smile. So, I
rit.

Freely
B♭
F/C
A7sus/E
A7
Dm
F7
march a lit - tle far - ther when I hear the long roll start _ for the
B♭
Csus
N.C.
reg - i - men - tal drum - mer in my heart. _
a tempo
B♭
F/A
Gm
F/A
B♭
F/A
E♭(9)
rit.

THE HONOR OF YOUR NAME

Lyrics by
JACK MURPHY

Music by
FRANK WILDHORN

B♭
G
a face I've nev-er seen be-fore. And Bill, I nev-er will for-get him.
I've learned to sow; I'll learn to plow. And Bill, I nev-er will for-get you.
C
C/B
Am
I knew at once that you were gone. He tipped his hat, and then moved on
The kids and I might move out West. I'll take our dream and leave the rest.
B♭
F
and left my world a cold and emp-ty space, such a lone-ly place.
There's noth-in' for my bro-ken heart to do 'cept write these words to you.
F/G
G
Chorus:
C
But for the prom-ise that we made
For the prom-ise that we made
-ise that we made
(mf)

G
C
C/B
Am
so long a - go, for the nights when you held me in your
so long a - go, for the love, all the love that will not
so long a - go, for the man that I see in our son's
F
C
E
Am
C7
To Coda
arms,
die,
eyes,
I will keep life's frag - ile flame for the
F
C/E
F/G
1.
Csus
C
2.
Csus
C
C/E
3
hon - or of your name.
name.
cresc.
Bridge:
F
G
C
May - be some - day, when I'm strong - er,

F
G
Am
I will look back on this day
G/B
F/C
C
and un - der - stand all the rea - sons why the
B♭
F/G
G
D.S. 𝄋 al Coda
good Lord took you a - way. But for the prom-
cresc.
𝄌 Coda
F
C/E
F/G
N.C.
Slowly
F/C
C
hon - or of your name.
rit. e dim.
rit.

IN GREAT DEEDS

Text by
JOSHUA LAWRENCE CHAMBERLAIN

Music by
FRANK WILDHORN

Monologue:
In great deeds something abides. On great fields something stays.
Forms change and pasts, bodies disappear, but spirits linger to consecrate ground for the vision place of the soul.
And reverent men and women from afar and generations that know us not and that we know not of shall come here to ponder and to dream.
And the power of the vision shall pass into their souls.

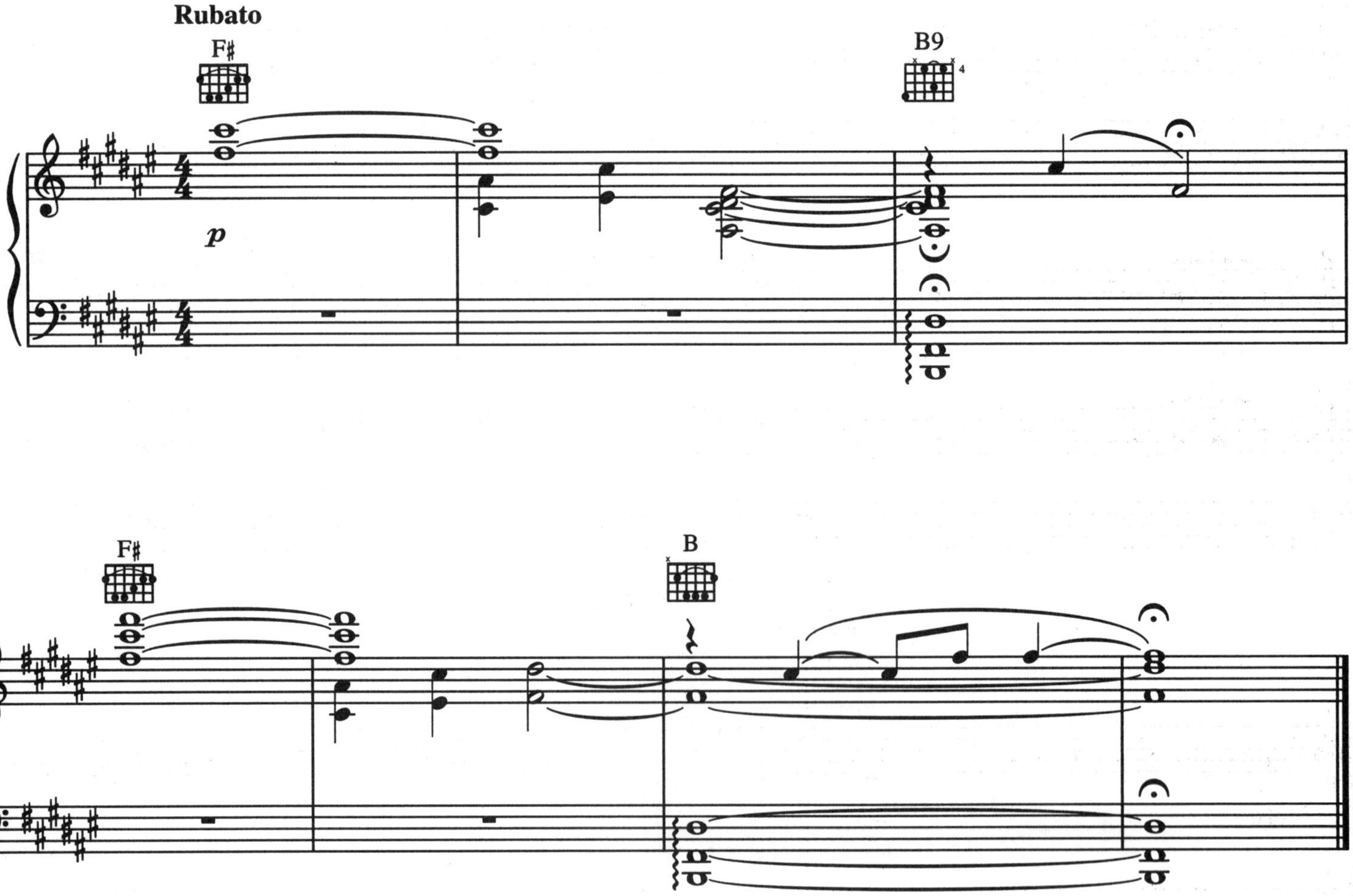

LAST WALTZ FOR DIXIE

Lyrics by
JACK MURPHY

Music by
FRANK WILDHORN

*Recorded a half step higher.

D/A A E
E♭/B♭ B♭ F
hands, we shall sur - ren - der to his glo - ry. And
nev - er been a group of men so splen - did, or a
D/A A C♯m E7
E♭/B♭ B♭ Dm F7
when they tell the sto - ry, let them say of the sons of the
cause so well de - fend - ed as our own, be it heav - en or
A Adim7 A/B
B♭ Bdim7 B♭/C
gray, not one turned a - way.
hell; hail and fare - well.
It's the

Chorus:
E G♯m A D/A A
Am B♭ E♭/B♭ B♭
last waltz for Dix - ie. It's the
E G♯m A
F Am B♭
last song she'll sing. So play it with
E 1. G♯ C♯m E7
F A Dm F7
pride for all those who died. And the spir - it in -
A E/G♯ A/B Esus E
B♭ F/A B♭/C Fsus F
side you, that's the Dix-ie in me. I be -

2. 3.
G♯ C♯m E7 To Coda A E/G♯
A Dm F7 B♭ F/A
all those who died. And the spir - it in - side you, that's the
A/B E Bridge: B/A E/G♯
B♭/C F C/B♭ F/A
Dix - ie in me. For all we hold dear, the
B/A G♯m A E/G♯
C/B♭ Am B♭ F/A
road a - head is clear. For all the things we hon - or, the

F♯/A♯
A/B
D.S. 𝄋 al Coda
G/B
B♭/C
mo - ment is here. It's the
Coda
A
E/G♯
Freely
A/B
B♭
F/A
B♭/C
side you, that's the Dix - ie in
rit.
Moderately
E
G♯m7
N.C.
F
Am7
me. (Last waltz for
A
E/G♯
F♯m
E
B♭
F/A
Gm
F
Dix - ie.) That's the Dix - ie in me.
rit.